D0598204

115618597

Christmas in Brazil

**Brazilians in Bahia enjoy the delightful
summer weather as they offer gifts to
Iemanjá, the goddess of the sea, on
December 31.**

Christmas in Brazil

**Christmas Around the World
From World Book**

World Book, Inc.
a Scott Fetzer company
Chicago London Sydney Toronto

Christmas in Brazil was prepared by the Editorial and Art Departments of World Book Publishing.

Copyright © 1991
World Book, Inc.
525 W. Monroe St.
Chicago, IL 60661

ISBN 0-7166-0891-X
Library of Congress Catalog Card Number 91-65934
Printed in the United States of America

Portions of *Christmas in Brazil* were printed on recycled paper.

The publisher wishes to thank the many individuals who took part in developing this publication.

Writer: Rebecca A. Lauer
Researcher: Kathryn Blatt
Consultants: Dirce Guerra Bottallo, Alvaro Marins de Almeida, Liana Pérola Schipper, and Braulio Tavares.

Special thanks go to Marilúcia and Fabio Bottallo, Astrid Cabral, Selma Monroe, Nilson C. Nas Cimento, and Ariani B. Friedl.

2 3 4 5 6 7 8 9 10 99 98 97 96 95 94

Contents

Chapter 1

A Festive Time of Year

For most of us, the word *Christmas* conjures up images of snowy landscapes, frosty mornings, sleigh bells, and snowmen. But mention Christmas to a Brazilian, and a different picture emerges. A Brazilian may talk about attending an outdoor midnight Mass or celebrating Christmas Day with a barbecue or a pig roast. The children may talk about plans for spending their summer vacation from school swimming and sunbathing.

In Brazil, Christmas arrives at the beginning of summer. There's no snow, no freezing temperatures, and no need to bundle up the little ones in warm clothes. From December through March—Brazilian summertime—temperatures range from 70 °F to more than 100 °F (21 °C to 38 °C). This is the season when Brazilians enjoy outdoor activities such as picnicking and sailing. In Rio de Janeiro and other cities along the coast, office workers may take a walk to the beach on their lunch hour, while crowds of Christmas shoppers wearing shorts and T-shirts throng the streets. But in spite of the heat, Santa Claus—or *Papai Noel* as he is known in Brazil—wears the traditional fur-trimmed red suit, big black boots, and long white beard. No one seems to think it strange that Papai Noel greets children in the tropical heat all bundled up for winter. It's just one of the

Christmas shoppers in lightweight clothes crowd a street in downtown São Paulo.

7

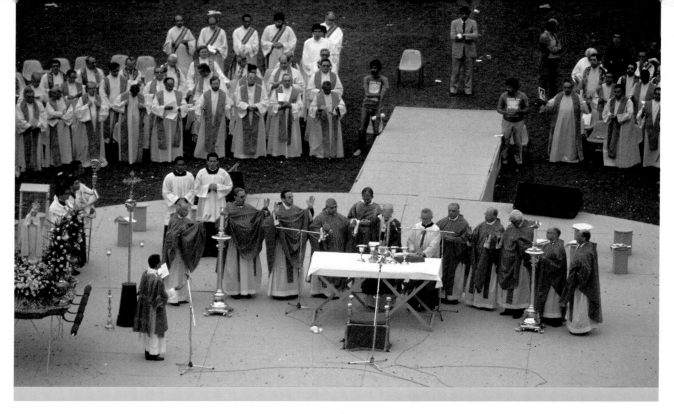

Many worshipers in Brazil attend open-air masses. This one was held at Maracanã Stadium in Rio de Janeiro.

delightful contradictions so characteristic of Brazil and its customs.

These contradictions result in part from importing European traditions to a tropical country. The Christmas season, as it is celebrated in Brazil today, is a colorful mixture of Portuguese-Catholic, African, and Indian traditions.

Hundreds of years ago, the Portuguese brought Christmas to Brazil, and Portuguese traditions still dominate the nation's Christmas celebrations today. However, the native Indian population and the descendants of the Africans brought to Brazil as slaves have also had an impact on the nation's Christmas customs.

The Indian and African influence is reflected primarily in the celebration of the Twelve Days of Christmas, from December 25th through January 6th—Three Kings' Day. During this

time, Brazilians participate in a range of activities that reflect the different origins of Brazil's people. On Christmas Eve, many people attend the Roman Catholic midnight Mass known as the *Missa do Galo* (Mass of the Rooster). One week later, on New Year's Eve, many Brazilians flock to Copacabana beach and participate in an African spiritualist ceremony that honors Iemanjá, the goddess of the sea.

These different ceremonies and religious observances are a result of the merging of many cultures. Over the centuries, the dominant Portuguese group intermarried with the African and Indian peoples to create a distinctly unique—and Brazilian—national character. To fully understand the range and spirit of the Brazilian Christmas season, it is helpful to know something about these people, their history, and the land in which they live.

In 1500, Portuguese explorer Pedro Álvares Cabral landed on the coast of Brazil and, thinking it was an island, claimed it for Portugal. During the 1530's, Portuguese colonists began to settle Brazil, and by 1549, a colonial government was established in the region. The colonists in the northeast soon established large sugar plantations. The Portuguese controlled Brazil until 1630, when the Dutch invaded what is now the state of Pernambuco. In 1654, however, the Portuguese ousted the Dutch and regained control. Portugal then ruled Brazil from afar until 1807, when France invaded Portugal, forcing the Portuguese royal family to flee to Brazil. Portuguese emperors then ruled the nation from Rio de Janeiro until 1889, when it was declared a republic. Since then, Brazil has had a succession of governments and suffered much political unrest and upheaval. Today, Brazil is a Federal Republic, with a civilian government consisting of a president, a congress, and a court system. However, the centuries of Portuguese dominance have had a profound influence on every aspect of Brazilian life.

Portuguese is the official language of Brazil. The name *Brazil* came from the Portuguese word *pau-brasil,* the name for a kind of tree native to the country.

When Brazilians wish each other "Merry Christmas," they say it in Portuguese: *Feliz Natal.* Portuguese is a Romance language—based on Latin, the language of the ancient Romans. It is related to Spanish, Italian, and French, and it is beautiful when spoken.

The Portuguese also introduced their religion to Brazil. Today, Brazil has the largest Catholic population of any country in the world—about 85 per cent of the people are Roman Catholic. Christmas is one of the holiest days of the year in Brazil. Nativity scenes depicting the birth of Jesus Christ grace churches and cathedrals, and most Brazilian homes have their own treasured Nativity scenes as well.

Long before the arrival of the Portuguese, a substantial Indian population lived in what is now Brazil. Anthropologists believe these people probably came from Asia or the Pacific Islands. Hunters and farmers, these native Indians are the only true Brazilians. Although their numbers have dwindled to only about 200,000, they represent the largest Indian population in Latin America today.

Beginning in the late 1500's, the Portuguese brought African slaves to work on their sugar

VENEZUELA · GUYANA · FRENCH GUIANA
COLOMBIA · SURINAME
Equator
Amazon River
North Atlantic Ocean
AMAZON REGION
NORTHEAST REGION
BRAZIL
PERU
Brasília
BOLIVIA
CENTRAL AND SOUTHERN PLATEAUS
Rio de Janeiro
São Paulo
South Pacific Ocean · CHILE · PARAGUAY
ARGENTINA
South Atlantic Ocean
URUGUAY

Rain Forest

Brazil occupies more than half the continent of South America, and has more people than all the other South American nations combined.

and coffee plantations. Over the years, intermarriage resulted in the blending of these various cultures. The arrival of Poles, Germans, Italians, and Japanese and other Asians in the 1800's added to the ethnic mix and, today, Brazil is one of the largest "melting pots" in the world. The nation has a population of 150 million people distributed over a far-reaching and varied landscape.

The largest country in South America, Brazil is also home to the world's biggest tropical rain forest. Mountains border the

forests in the north and the Atlantic Ocean in the southeast. The mighty Amazon River winds through the green jungles of the interior. Dry plains and low plateaus lie in northeast, central and southern Brazil. Fabulous beaches and fine harbors stretch along Brazil's 6,019 miles (9,687 kilometers) of coastline, attracting thousands of tourists every year.

Brazil's land area is larger than the continental United States. In such a vast country, regional variations on the traditional Christmas theme abound. In the south, for instance, where pine trees grow in abundance, most people decorate a real tree for Christmas. But in northern Brazil, where pine trees are rare, most people buy an artificial Christmas tree rather than import a fresh one. However, the basic traditions do not vary, and Christmas is celebrated with typical Brazilian enthusiasm in every part of the country.

Christmas in Brazil, inherited as it is from the Portuguese, is much like Christmas in America and Europe. Christmas cards are sent, gifts are exchanged, and shops and malls are decorated with festive displays. Brilliant Christmas lights brighten the city streets. In Brazilian homes, where the Nativity scene is a must, a lavish Christmas feast is served and Santa Claus brings the children gifts. For many Brazilians, Christmas is a private and holy occasion shared with close friends and family.

Brazilians celebrate Christmas with the same vibrant enthusiasm that they bring to all their festivities. Brazilians are renowned for their lively, free-spirited, and colorful celebrations, including the famous Carnival—a four-day pre-Lenten festival that is said to be the most spectacular event of its kind. As a people, the Brazilians have elevated having a good time into an art form, dancing and singing into the night with seemingly boundless energy.

Brazilians are spontaneous, affectionate, and lively as well as easygoing and informal. For example, Brazilians think little of showing up an hour late for an appointment, and it seems they are never too busy to pick up a simple six-string guitar or some other musical instrument and have an impromptu party. This spontaneous spirit is part of the Brazilian character—a character formed by the blending of a wide variety of races and cultures.

Many Brazilians attend midnight Mass, where priests tell the age-old story of the coming of Christ, the meaning of Christmas, and the need for universal peace and brotherhood. Midnight services are often very

Brasília, the capital of Brazil, is decorated for Christmas with thousands of strings of tiny white lights.

beautiful—the churches are lit with hundreds of candles and decorated with flowers, wreaths, and garlands.

After midnight Mass, the children are put to bed, and the adults often stay up till all hours of the night, drinking coffee, enjoying conversation, or joining in music and song. Brazilians are a very musical people, famous for introducing the *bossa nova* (new beat) to the world. And Christmas is a special holiday—the birthday of the infant Jesus. This holy day is celebrated in true Brazilian style, with singing and possibly some dancing as well. And if the festivities last all night long—that's Christmas in Brazil!

Chapter 2

The Celebrations Begin

Christmas in Brazil is a festive season arriving at a festive time of year—summer. Combined with the Brazilian enthusiasm for celebrations, the tropical temperatures make Christmas in Brazil unique—a special time with a magic all its own.

Like people in Europe and North America, Brazilians start preparing for Christmas well in advance of the holiday. The first signs of Christmas appear early in December when the streets and office buildings of the larger Brazilian cities are dressed up with Christmas lights and decorations. At night, cities such as Rio de Janeiro, São Paulo, and Brasília—the capital of Brazil—glitter with white and multi-colored Christmas lights. During the day, window displays in the shops and malls announce that Christmas is just around the corner.

These displays range from a simple Christmas tree painted on a window to elaborate creations that rival those seen in department store windows in America and Europe. Some displays include life-sized figures of the Holy Family, with the Three Wise Men offering gifts. The figures of the Wise Men may be animated, moving back and forth to offer frankincense and myrrh to the Christ Child. *Papai Noel*, with his reindeer and elves, may also be animated.

Papai Noel pauses to accept a treat from a young girl on the street in Rio de Janeiro.

Brazilians and tourists alike may make a special trip downtown to see these enchanting displays.

It isn't until the middle of December, however, that Christmas preparations—and celebrations—begin in earnest. One of the most spectacular events is the arrival of Papai Noel. Every year, around the middle of December, thousands of children gather in Maracanã Stadium, Rio de Janeiro's largest stadium, to watch and wait for Papai

Noel. He's definitely on his way—but not in a sleigh pulled by reindeer. Brazil's Papai Noel arrives by helicopter. He lands in the middle of a colorful landing pad, amid loud cries and shouts.

The children, who can contain themselves no longer, break away from their parents and run to greet Papai Noel. He is quickly surrounded by thousands of wide-eyed, happy children. After shaking their hands and

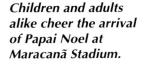

Children and adults alike cheer the arrival of Papai Noel at Maracanã Stadium.

Children reenact the Nativity scene during an outdoor play at Maresias Beach.

wishing them "Boas Festas," Papai Noel passes out gifts. The children receive water pistols, balloons, whistles, or other small toys.

Afterward, Papai Noel makes his way to the nearby stage—it's time for a sing-along. Accompanied by local singers and musicians, Papai Noel starts to sing and the crowd joins in. Maracanã Stadium is filled with the sounds of Christmas carols, popular Brazilian tunes, and favorite children's songs. Although the largest event of this kind takes place in Rio de Janeiro, Papai Noel arrives by helicopter in other large cities too. It is an event that draws people from miles around, and the children look forward to it every year. Many of them will remember it for years to come.

Another impressive tradition in Brazil is the *Auto de Natal,* or Act of Christmas, an outdoor Christmas play held every year in Rio de Janeiro. Although it has been part of Rio's Christmas festivities for only about ten years, it has a devoted following and draws a large crowd. Every year thousands of *Cariocas,* as the people of Rio are called, come to see this colorful drama The Auto de Natal is usually held in downtown Rio in a large outdoor theater called the Arcos da Lapa. Admission is free, so even the poorest Carioca can enjoy this Christmas play. In fact, the play is usually about poor children living in Brazil today, and these heart-warming pageants serve as a reminder of the true meaning of Christmas.

In a country where Roman Catholicism predominates, the religious aspect of Christmas is very strong. Nowhere is this more apparent than in the *presépios,* or Nativity scenes, that are displayed throughout Brazil.

Christmas in Brazil wouldn't be Christmas without the Nativity scene—one of the most im-portant of all Brazilian tradi-tions. All the churches and al-most every Brazilian home puts up a presépio.

In the northern regions, where the Catholic faith is espe-cially strong, the presépio is far more important than either Papai Noel or the Christmas tree. For northern people, Christ's birth is the real celebra-tion, and since the presépio rep-resents that event, it holds a place of honor in their homes.

In the great cathedrals and churches of Brazil, the presé-pios may be life-sized statues of

Brazilian presépios come in all shapes and sizes. This life-size outdoor presépio is in Florianopolis, in the state of Santa Catarina.

Jesus, the Virgin Mary, Joseph, and the Three Kings. Life-sized animals, such as sheep and donkeys, may also be included. There may also be a rooster, to signify the *Missa do Galo,* or Mass of the Rooster.

The manger is often made out of wood, with straw lining the floor, a reminder of the Christ Child's birth in a stable. The presépios in churches, which depict the traditional Nativity scene, are so splendid that even people who are not religiously inclined go to church to see them.

It is in Brazilian homes, however, that some of the most original creations are found. Many of these presépios are also very elaborate. Some are heirlooms that have been in one family for generations, handed down from mother to daughter. It is not unusual for a Brazilian family to have a presépio that belonged to a great-grandmother or even a great-great-grandmother.

A typical Brazilian family presépio includes figures of the Holy Family, the Magi, and perhaps an angel, a star, some cows, chickens and sheep— and, of course, a rooster.

The mother often places the presépio on her best embroidered tablecloth. Every family member is then free to add his or her own personal touch to this basic scene. Young boys

may decide to surround Jesus and the shepherds with an electric train or perhaps a plane. Girls may add a swan or a sailboat. Many animals native to Brazil find their way into the Nativity scene, such as tigers and alligators about to pounce on sheep. Even the mythical and wild Amazon *onça,* or jaguar, is included. The end result is a colorful Nativity scene that

The mild weather at Christmastime in Brazil makes outdoor presépios popular. Here, a family sets up a Nativity scene in their garden.

blends the old and the new, the innovative and the traditional. These anachronisms do not seem to bother Brazilians. Instead, it is as if they are offering up all of human achievement to the Holy Child, incorporating both past and present.

In some regions of Brazil, the people add Brazilian fruits to their Nativity scenes. Never mind that these tropical fruits were never seen in Bethlehem. Pineapples, bananas, and red mangoes are placed on the desert sand, or even inside the

Old meets new in this Brazilian home, where a neon decoration tops a tree surrounded by folk arts and crafts.

These schoolchildren celebrate the upcoming holiday in a classroom party. The children are no doubt happily anticipating their impending summer vacation as well.

manger with the Baby Jesus. For Brazilians, this makes the presépio more colorful and interesting.

Many Brazilian presépios are handmade every year, using everyday household items. Mountains are made out of papier-mâché or even out of paper bags from the grocery store. A mirror may serve as a lake, with the handle covered in straw to maintain the illusion. A china goose may be placed on the mirror to create an interesting reflection. Bright-colored sawdust becomes desert sand or the floor of the manger. Small pieces of fresh pine trees are added, as well as miniature arti-

ficial trees. In the northern regions, mountains and figures might be created from clay and earthenware. Especially ambitious Brazilians create new figures of the Holy Family every year. These may be lightly painted, or dressed in doll clothes. The overall effect may be simple or splendid, depending upon the skill of the builders.

Many Brazilian presépios are works of art—beautifully arranged, with every detail in place. Still others may look somewhat comical because no two figures are the same size— the baby Jesus may tower over his parents, or a sheep may be much larger than a camel. How-

Dwarfed by an elaborate tree, these shoppers in São Paulo are looking for just the right gifts for family and friends.

ever, such details do not concern the Brazilians. Creating the presépio is a national pastime, and if everyone has a good time making the Nativity scene, that's all that counts.

Certainly the children enjoy themselves immensely, adding their own artistic touches to the family presépio. In some families, the Nativity scene may be so large that it fills a whole room, while others are small and simple. Most fall somewhere in-between, and would fit comfortably on a coffee table. Frequently, the presépio is placed near the Christmas tree.

In some parts of Brazil, the presépio is set up early in December, while in others, especially in the south, it is not put up until the day before Christmas. And if the scene is elaborate, one or two family members may spend all day working on it to make sure that the presépio is ready by Christmas Eve. No matter what the end result is, the presépio is cherished by everyone. Most family members have taken part in its creation, even if only to add a pine branch or a toy windmill, and so everyone feels a strong sense of pride in their Nativity scene.

Many children take an even more active role in this ancient religious drama by participating in school Nativity plays. These amateur dramas bring the age-old story of Mary, Jesus, and Joseph alive for children and parents alike. Not only do the children enjoy dressing up as these important personages, but parents and teachers find it is an effective way to teach young people about the true meaning of Christmas.

In addition, many Brazilians observe the religious aspects of Christmas by giving to the poor and underprivileged. The Roman Catholic Church sponsors many fund-raising events at Christmas, often in conjunction with other church organizations and Protestant missions. This unity is especially appropriate since Christmas Day in Brazil is officially known as the day of spiritual union among all churches.

All these fund-raisers help ensure that the poor, especially the children, have a better Christmas. People from all walks of life attend bingo games and raffles to raise money for toys and gifts. Everyone seems to enjoy these affairs, which are often held outdoors. The atmosphere is frequently like that of a festival and there is usually an abundance of flowers, music, and flags. Gifts may be distributed right on the spot to those in need. The money raised is used to provide Christmas dinner and

practical gifts for orphans and the poor. These events are usually a success, because it is a tradition in Brazil to give something, no matter how small, to those less fortunate. Even if someone can only afford to give enough to pay for a potato or a little rice, it is welcome. There is always someone in greater need who will appreciate the gift.

Christmas is the season for giving, and like people in Christian countries all over the world, Brazilians go Christmas shopping for their friends and family. The search for the right gift begins in earnest at the beginning of December. No one wants to wait until the last moment.

Because of Brazil's extremely high rate of inflation, gifts may not be extravagant. A family of modest means might buy their children basic necessities like shoes and clothing, while those who are more comfortable might surprise their children with books, electric trains, dolls, and games.

A law in Brazil known as the "13th salary" or "Christmas bonus" helps make Christmas more affordable for everyone. This law ensures that every Brazilian worker receives an extra month's pay at Christmastime. Sometimes half of the "13th salary" will be distributed in November, and the other half in December. Introduced in the

Children draw slips of paper to see whose "secret friend" they will be.

After days of wondering and waiting, these children finally get to open their Amigo Secreto gifts.

early 1960's when President João Goulart was in office, it is a popular law in Brazil. The "13th salary" gives people the extra money they need for Christmas gifts and celebrations. It is a welcome addition to the family income.

In recent years, a gift-giving tradition known as *Amigo Secreto* or "Secret Friend" has become popular. In this tradition, a group of friends, co-workers, schoolchildren, or family members write their names on pieces of paper and put the names in a bowl. Then everyone draws a name. No one reveals who their "secret friend" is. It's strictly confidential. Then each person buys a gift for the person whose name they drew. On Christmas Eve, when the gifts are opened, people find out who drew their

name. However, office workers may open their gifts a few days before Christmas, and schoolchildren may exchange gifts before school closes for summer vacation.

Often the Amigo Secreto gifts are "gag" gifts, and office workers and schoolchildren may try to see who can give the most outrageous presents. Often, the gift is something that obviously does not fit the person it was selected for, such as tiny clothes for a six-foot-tall man, or cigars for a non-smoker. Everyone has a good time laughing along with the person who has received the funniest gift. Sometimes there are two rounds of gifts—the first with funny gifts, the second with more appropriate ones.

At this time of year, Brazilians are also busy writing and

sending Christmas cards to friends and acquaintances. True to the traditional European Christmas, many Brazilian Christmas cards still show winter scenes. Numerous cards depict Santa with his reindeer, gliding across snow a foot deep. Many cards show Christmas trees covered with snowflakes, or children bundled up in warm clothes, even though these scenes do not reflect Christmas in Brazil.

This custom is beginning to change, and it is now possible to find Christmas cards with sandy beaches and palm trees, or Christmas trees without snow. But even though these are more representative of Brazil, most Brazilians still send traditional Christmas cards with scenes of a white Christmas.

Following another interesting custom, Brazilians may not send their cards out until after Christmas. In Brazil, Christmas greetings encompass the entire twelve days of Christmas— from December 25th through January 6th, Three Kings' Day. So receiving a card from a friend after both Christmas and New Year's Day have passed is common.

Of course, many Brazilians do send their cards so that they arrive closer to the holidays, but no apologies are made—or needed—for belated greetings. Most carry the message *"Boas Festas,"* or "Happy Holidays," and are welcomed at any time during the twelve days of Christmas.

As the days get closer to Christmas, Brazilians start to think about putting up their Christmas trees. In some families and in some parts of the country, the tree is put up a week before Christmas. In southern Brazil, however, the tree is not put up until Christmas Eve.

The tree itself and the decorations also vary from region to region. In northern Brazil, for example, pine trees are rare, so most people put up artificial trees. These trees are generally small, and come in every color. They may be gold, silver, blue, white, red, or even purple, and they are usually set on a small table. These artificial Christmas trees are decorated with bright metallic ornaments of every color, and an angel is often placed on the very top of the tree. Beautifully crafted hand-made ornaments such as clay figurines are also hung on the tree, and bright-red poinsettias add even more color. Even though it is warm and balmy in Brazil, the decorations suggest the traditional white Christmas. Puffs of white cotton on the branches of the tree—and often

People shop for live Christmas trees at this plants fair in São Paulo.

under it as well—make it look like snow has fallen.

In the south of Brazil, many of the same decorations are used, but real pine trees are plentiful in the south. People go out and select their tree, just as people do in the eastern and northern areas of the United States. However, few people chop down their own tree. They generally buy one from a vendor. Their trees are usually large, stretching from floor to ceiling, and they are often decorated with real candles—placed very carefully in special holders that protect the pine needles from the flames. Beautifully lit with dozens of flickering candles, such a Christmas tree can make a whole room come alive. With the addition of metallic balls, poinsettias, and handmade figurines, the result is spectacular.

In the southern region of Brazil, decorating the tree is primarily the job of the parents. Usually the mother and father set up the tree behind locked doors, and the children aren't allowed to see it until it is finished. For the children, of course, the anticipation is almost unbearable. Some may try peeking through the keyhole to get a glimpse. But at last all the candles are lit, and the children are allowed to see the Christmas tree in all its splendor.

In most other regions of Brazil, the tree is put up at least a week before Christmas, and the whole family helps decorate it. Everyone in the family gets a chance to hang an ornament or place a bright-red poinsettia flower on the tree.

This time of year is especially exciting for children—it is only a matter of days now before Papai Noel arrives and there will be gifts under the tree. If the children didn't get the chance to see Papai Noel when he arrived by helicopter, they will certainly pay him a visit in the last week or two before Christmas. All over Brazil, Papai Noel can be seen at local shopping areas and malls. Even in rural areas, children can go and sit on Papai Noel's lap.

To many children in Brazil, Papai Noel is not just a mythical, mysterious character who brings presents on Christmas Eve and is never seen or heard. Papai Noel is a real personality to most Brazilian children, perhaps because of his frequent appearances. Parents often hire people—or ask their friends—to dress up as Papai Noel and pay the children a visit. It's no wonder many children feel like they know Papai Noel personally.

As Christmas draws nearer, only days away, everyone makes last-minute preparations. There are still a few gifts to buy, and new clothes and shoes must be purchased for the children. Many adults also want to wear something new to the Missa do Galo. The ingredients for the Christmas feast must be purchased, and the house must be cleaned.

Many Brazilians decide to treat themselves to a *cesta de Natal,* or Christmas basket. The cestas de Natal are colorful, festive baskets made of wood and straw and stuffed with practically every kind of food and drink required for a scrumptious Christmas feast. The basket may contain fine wine, champagne, or whiskey, and irresistible treats such as chocolates, nuts, and sweets. Dried fruits and canned goods nestle under the colorful cellophane wrapping. The baskets come in every price range—from the simple and inexpensive to the elaborate and costly. Almost everyone can find something affordable.

Preparing for the Christmas feast also means buying a turkey—a traditional Christmas dish for many Brazilians. In the rural areas, an old tradition calls for feeding a live turkey a sugary rum called *cachaça.* This is

A young girl play-fully gives Papai Noel's beard a tug in this department store in São Paulo.

done on the day before Christmas to tenderize the meat. The turkey is allowed to drink the cachaça until it is full. When the turkey has consumed a large amount, it is promptly killed.

Brazilians have many sayings that stem from this tradition. For example, if a person is unduly worried about a problem or situation, a friend might say, "Only the turkey dies the day before." This idiomatic saying means, "Don't worry. Things always happen in their proper time." Another saying related to this tradition is, "To die the day before like a turkey." This means to be anxious, to be in a very bad way.

By the time the turkey is purchased for Christmas dinner, Christmas Eve may be only a day or two away. Soon it will be time to open presents. Soon everyone will get together with friends and family. Relatives may be driving from distant regions to spend Christmas with the family. Older children will get to stay up late and attend midnight Mass. Adults will raise a toast with wine or champagne. The huge Christmas feast will be enjoyed by all. This is one of the most eagerly awaited times of the year, especially for the children. Christmas will soon be here.

Chapter 3

Christmas Eve and the

Mass of
the Rooster

Brazil is a country where regional differences abound, but two Christmas customs are universally practiced on Christmas Eve throughout this vast nation. The first is the Christmas dinner, or *ceia de Natal.* The second is the midnight Mass, known in Brazil as the *Missa do Galo,* or Mass of the Rooster.

Many people host an elaborate Christmas dinner around 10 or 11 o'clock at night, and then go to midnight Mass. In some regions, Christmas dinner is not served until after the Missa do Galo, which makes for a very late night indeed.

Christmas Eve in Brazil is very much a family affair—a time when relatives get together to share Christmas dinner. All the married children may converge on their parents' house with their own brood of children, so that grandparents and grandchildren can celebrate together. People who live far away from their family may spend the evening with friends until it's time to go to church. Christmas Eve is also the time when *Papai Noel* visits the children.

For most Brazilians, December 24th is a very busy day. Everyone takes part in the preparations. If the presépio is not already set up, the father starts early and works on it all day to get it ready for Christmas Eve. The house is given a last-minute sprucing up. The best silverware and china are

This elegant presépio is a focal point during the Missa do Galo in this church in São Paulo.

cleaned and polished. The children lay out the new clothes they will wear to Christmas dinner. And the mother has the awesome responsibility of cooking Christmas dinner—no small task by anyone's standards.

Most Brazilian women enjoy cooking, and they start preparing the Christmas feast early in the day. They make a special *farofa* stuffing for the turkey—a dressing that is very different from the kinds of stuffing served in northern Europe and America. Farofa is made with manioc flour, which comes from a starchy, potato-like root that is a staple in the Brazilian Indian diet. Long before the Portuguese introduced their traditions to Brazil, the Indians used the manioc root to make flour, bread, and cakes, and manioc flour has been incorporated into many Brazilian dishes over the centuries. To make farofa, the manioc flour is first toasted. Turkey liver and gizzard, onions, garlic, hard-boiled eggs, olives,

Everyone pitches in to help Mom create a spectacular *ceia de Natal*.

and bacon are then added, and this mixture is used to stuff the turkey.

Many years ago, dried cod was the traditional main course at Christmas, but roast turkey has become popular over the last 10 to 20 years. Of course, individual family preferences differ, and some opt instead to serve a small pork roast or even the traditional cod instead. Many Brazilian families, especially the more affluent ones, serve all three dishes.

The dried cod is prepared according to Portuguese custom in a sort of fish cake known as *bolinho de bacalhau*. The cod is diced, mixed with mashed potatoes, onions, sweet peppers, tomatoes, and olives, and then deep-fried. The bolinho de bacalhau, served in portions about the size of a muffin, is an extremely popular dish.

A great variety of side dishes and desserts are also prepared. Banana pudding is a favorite, and many native fruits, such as pineapples, grapes, and bananas, are found at the Brazilian Christmas feast. In fact, a common Brazilian gift in the north is a crate of grapes imported from the south.

No Brazilian Christmas feast would be complete, however, without a dessert called *rabanada*. Rabanada is very similar to French toast and is so well-liked

Candles, crystal, and silver adorn the table at this elegant Christmas Eve dinner.

that it has become a Brazilian institution. In addition to friendly competition that exists among cooks, there are formal contests to see who can make the best rabanada. At this time of year, it is customary to serve this Brazilian specialty to guests, and every Brazilian host keeps a supply of rabanada on hand for visitors.

Rabanada is made with large loaves of French bread specially prepared in bakeries during the Christmas season for use in this delicious dessert. The bread is purchased 24 hours ahead of time and left out all night to make it hard and stale enough to slice easily. Each slice is then dipped in a mixture of milk and

These people take an opportunity to wish Season's Greetings to their neighbors.

beaten eggs, deep-fried until golden brown, and sprinkled with cinnamon and sugar before serving. Sometimes port wine is used instead of milk. Rabanada is easy to prepare and tastes very much like baked cinnamon rolls—small wonder it's a favorite throughout Brazil.

Other popular desserts at the traditional Christmas feast include Christmas cookies, honey cookies, mousse, and ice cream. Some desserts are made from family recipes that have been handed down through the generations. These desserts may be known only as "Grandma's pudding" or "Marilúcia's pudding," named for the person who originated the recipe.

Brazilian Christmas feasts also feature nuts of all kinds. Traditionally, walnuts and chestnuts were imported from Portugal and Spain, because the early settlers and their descendants wanted to celebrate Christmas with foods that reminded them of home. But in recent years, domestically grown nuts such as cashews and Brazil nuts have become popular, since they are more plentiful and less costly than imported nuts. These nuts and other snacks are often set out in the early evening. Visitors may drop in, and everyone needs something to nibble on until it's time to sit down to dinner.

In São Paulo, the industrial center of Brazil, it is customary to visit neighbors on Christmas Eve. Around 6 or 7 o'clock in the evening, many young people go door-to-door wishing their neighbors *Boas Festas,* or Merry Christmas, with much hugging, kissing, and well-wishing. Many people invite the merrymakers in to celebrate the holiday with wine or coffee, Christmas cookies, and nuts.

The atmosphere is warm and festive, and it's a good time to share the spirit of Christmas with neighbors. Brazilians are a very sociable people, and variations of this neighborly tradition are practiced in smaller towns and rural areas all over the country. Shortly after 7 o'clock, the well-wishers head home to be with their immediate family.

In the southern regions of Brazil, another very special event takes place on Christmas Eve. Around 8 o'clock, behind closed doors, the parents light the candles on the Christmas tree. There may be dozens of candles, and no artificial lights at all. The excitement grows as the children wait impatiently for their parents to finish lighting the candles. It is a magical moment when at last the Christmas tree is ready and the door is opened. Few things are as beautiful as a room illuminated with candlelight, and when all those candles light up a decorated Christmas tree, the effect is breathtaking for children and adults alike.

Afterward, the whole family may join in singing Christmas songs around the tree. *"Noite Feliz"* or "Silent Night" and *"Boas Festas"* are among the favorites. "Boas Festas," a song

The members of this Brazilian family raise their glasses in a holiday toast.

written by Brazilian composer Assis Valente, tells how poor children feel during the Christmas season. Many children sing this tune:

Anoiteceu, o sino bateu, a gente ficou feliz a rezar... eu pensai quo todo mundo fosse filho de Papai Noel...

(The night has fallen, the bells are tolling, and we were happy as we prayed. I used to think that everyone was Papai Noel's child.)

A toy car is one of many treats in the shoes of this young boy on Christmas morning.

In southern Brazil, Christmas Eve is also the time when Papai Noel makes house calls. Many parents hire people to dress up as Papai Noel and visit their children. Friends and co-workers may also be enlisted for this job. In any event, it is a wondrous experience for the children—here is Papai Noel in person, come just to visit them! They can actually talk to him, sit on his lap, and tell him how well-behaved they have been. More often than not, Papai Noel brings a huge sack full of gifts—and that is the best part of all! There are dolls for the girls and games and electric toys for the boys. Books and clothes are also popular gifts. Children in Brazil attack their presents like children do in North America—with great enthusiasm and no restraint whatsoever. Some especially perceptive children may recognize Papai Noel behind that beard, and realize that the gift-giver is really their next-door neighbor or their gardener, but no matter. He brings presents and a jolly spirit, and Christmas just wouldn't be Christmas without him.

In many other regions of Brazil, however, Papai Noel will probably not make an actual appearance. Instead, the children put their shoes beside the Christmas tree or by their bed. Some children put their shoes near the window. The shoes will be filled with gifts when the children awaken in the morning.

*The treats she found on Christmas
morning were well worth the wait
for this little girl.*

The Brazilian version of Santa Claus never comes down the chimney, because there are few chimneys in Brazil—the warm climate makes them unnecessary. Papai Noel simply walks in the front door with his gifts.

In other families, the parents hide the children's presents outdoors, and the children search for them—much as children hunt for Easter eggs in America and other countries. Since the weather is warm in Brazil and there is no snow, Christmas gifts can be hidden outside without them getting wet or ruined.

Other families put the children's presents outside the door and pretend that Papai Noel left them there. Around midnight, the children find and open their brightly wrapped gifts.

In a country as vast as Brazil, there are many variations on the Christmas celebration, and individual families also have different customs, depending on their ancestry. For instance, a family with strong German origins has different Christmas traditions than a family with Portuguese or Italian roots. São Paulo has a large Italian and Japanese population, while Santa Catarina, a state in southern Brazil, was largely settled by Germans. Many people of Polish descent live in the southern states of Paraná and Rio Grande do Sul. Thus, Brazil's history helps explain some of the regional variations in its customs. However, all the people share the spirit of Christmas. To Brazilians everywhere, Christmas is a very special and holy celebration. In most families, the festivities begin early on Christmas Eve and culminate with the ceia de Natal, or Christmas dinner, and midnight Mass.

The ceia de Natal is usually served around 10 o'clock at night, sometimes as late as 11 o'clock. Most Brazilian cooks have spent all day preparing the meal, and by now, the house is filled with delicious aromas that whet the appetite. Everyone sits down to a beautifully decorated table laden with rich, delicious food, including the traditional roast turkey with farofa dressing, dried cod, and various side dishes. Often a wide choice of desserts is offered, including the rabanada, and fruit is usually on the table—thinly sliced and attractively arranged. Wine and champagne flow freely for the adults, as well as a special Christmas punch made with Brazilian fruit juices.

Brazilians also appreciate an elaborately arranged table, and so there is often a handsome centerpiece on display. This may include multicolored can-

The lovely summer weather prompts this family to open their Christmas gifts outdoors.

dles in the shape of pears, bananas, and pineapples, or perhaps a wreath of hot red peppers and white garlic cloves. Or there may be a scene representative of Brazil and Christmas. The table is set with the family's best china, and only the finest glassware is used. The table is aglow in candlelight as the whole family gathers around to share this special Christmas dinner.

After everyone has eaten their fill of everything, it's time to go to the Missa do Galo. This midnight Mass was originated by Pope Saint Telesforo, in 143 A.D. The Pope ordered that three masses be celebrated—the first at midnight, the hour of Jesus' birth; the second at daybreak, the hour of the shepherds' veneration; and the third at sunrise. The name *Missa do Galo* may stem from the legend that of all the animals present when Christ was born, the rooster gave the world the first recognizable sign of the birth by crowing.

Since about 85 per cent of the people in Brazil are Roman Catholic, the Missa do Galo is well attended. This midnight Mass, one of the holiest Catholic services of the year, may last more than an hour. The Missa do Galo is often celebrated outdoors in a stage area or an open-air cathedral. The air is scented with incense and fragrant flowers. Adults and children alike join in the service by singing hymns and saying prayers aloud. In most services, the mass is said in Portuguese and so is understood by all. Usually only one priest says mass, but several priests may assist at the

For many, Christmas Eve ends with the Missa do Galo, as in this church in Florianopolis.

Christmas service. Services consist of readings from the Scripture and a Christmas sermon, and many people take Holy Communion in remembrance of Christ's Last Supper. In some churches, people leave gifts for the poor in front of the presépio. The children and adults sing as they proceed down the aisle, leaving their presents, wrapped in white, next to the Holy Child. In this way they are observing one of the basic teachings of Christmas—that it is just as rewarding to give as it is to receive.

While many people attend the Missa do Galo, some prefer to watch the Vatican services on television at home. In recent years, this custom has become popular in the large coastline cities of Rio de Janeiro and São Paulo. After their big Christmas dinner, many Brazilians prefer to relax at home and watch midnight Mass offered by the Pope himself. Every year at this time, the Vatican services are broadcast all over the world, and Brazilians are not the only ones tuning in. For many people, nothing can quite compare with watching the services from Rome. If they can't actually be at the Vatican, watching midnight Mass on television is the next best alternative—and it can

be enjoyed in the intimacy of the home.

After midnight Mass, many families simply go home to bed. The children put out their shoes for Papai Noel before going to sleep. Other families wait until after midnight Mass to enjoy their Christmas dinner. Even the children are allowed to stay up for midnight Mass and the ceia de Natal afterward.

In certain regions of Brazil, some families celebrate all night long—there is always plenty of wine and champagne available. Many people also drink *cafèzinho*—tiny cups of sweet, steaming-hot coffee—to help them stay awake. Along with the wine and cafèzinho, there is a constant flow of lively, light-hearted conversation—relatives from different cities have a lot of catching up to do. The warm weather often draws people outdoors, where they may sit and converse for hours on the backyard patio. Finally, in the wee hours of the morning, everyone says good night and drifts off to sleep at last. Tomorrow is, after all, Christmas Day. For some it will be a festive event; for others it will be a day to relax and unwind. Christmas morning is a time of great excitement for children who did not open their gifts on Christmas Eve. Some children find their gifts right beside their bed. Other children

Some families prefer to spend Christmas Day quietly, relaxing at home. Others get together with friends and neighbors for a lively barbecue.

find them under the tree. Now the children have new toys to play with and new clothes to wear.

For those families who had their Christmas dinner on Christmas Eve and attended midnight Mass, Christmas Day itself is fairly quiet and more subdued. Everyone has the day off, and this in itself makes Christmas Day enjoyable. Many young people living along the coast of Brazil spend the day at the beach. Others get together with friends to enjoy the national holiday.

In the southern regions of Brazil, however, Christmas Day may be celebrated in a different way. Those who did not attend midnight Mass may go to an early morning Christmas service instead. Later, several related families may get together for a huge barbecue. Everyone arrives around 11 o'clock in the morning, dressed very casually in shorts and T-shirts. A huge picnic table is set up to accommodate everyone. After the men get the grill started, skewers of beef, chicken, pork, or sausage are roasted over the open fire. Sometimes the more ambitious Brazilians dig a pit in their backyard and have a pig roast.

The men do the barbecuing, while the women prepare the side dishes and set the table. Lots of potato salad and tropical

fruits are served. The weather is ideal for a barbecue, hot and sunny, and the party lasts most of the day.

At last, Christmas Day draws to a close, and it is time to go home and get some rest—but not for long. Christmas may be over but the Christmas season is still in full swing. From December 24 through January 6, Three Kings' Day, there is almost nonstop activity throughout Brazil—not the least of which is the *Réveillon* or New Year's Eve celebration. And ushering in the New Year is the Feast of Iemanjá, a tribute to an African goddess of the sea. On New Year's Day, a colorful boat parade honors *Nossa Senhora dos Navegantes,* or Our Lady of Sailors. And throughout Brazil, various religious festivals mark the end of the year. While Christmas is a quiet and family-centered event, most of the New Year's festivities are colorful, frenzied, loud, and exuberant. Brazilians like nothing better than to set work aside and take part in a festival, and now, in the middle of the summer and the Christmas season, that's exactly what they do.

Chapter 4

Awakening the New Year

In Brazil, New Year's Eve is called the *Réveillon,* a name that comes from the French word *réveiller,* meaning "to awaken." The Réveillon, as the term is used in Brazil, literally means "to awaken the new year"—and Brazilians set out to do just that.

While Christmas in Brazil is a private and holy occasion, New Year's Eve is ushered in with a loud, public, and spectacular bang in a colorful mixture of American, European, and African celebrations. On this night there are a host of things to do, a wide variety of activities to enjoy.

All-night celebrations take place throughout Brazil, including formal balls and dinner parties in the cities, as well as more casual get-togethers in rural and urban areas alike. Along the coast, spectacular fireworks displays light up the beaches.

The city of São Paulo stages an international running marathon with a cast of thousands, while Rio de Janeiro offers an all-day and all-night festival in honor of Iemanjá, an African goddess of the sea. There's truly something for everyone in Brazil on this special night.

Many Brazilians believe that eating a portion of lentils exactly at midnight on New Year's Eve ensures prosperity for the upcoming year, so lentils are often found on New

Participants splash into the ocean during a festival to Iemanjá at Praia Grande in São Paulo.

Year's Eve menus and on buffet tables. Wearing new clothes on New Year's Eve is also a tradition in Brazil.

In the evening, some of the more affluent Brazilians enjoy spectacular balls and formal parties hosted by large hotels and nightclubs, or celebrate with friends at private parties. In the large cities, many people get all dressed up for the Réveillon festivities. The women wear colorful ballgowns or elaborate dresses with headdresses, some reminiscent of Carnival costumes. The men wear formal "black tie" attire.

Like New Year's Eve celebrations around the world, Brazil's Réveillon is a festive, all-night affair. Popular Brazilian music is played by lively musicians, while people toot on party horns and bright-colored confetti falls on the crowd. As the customary New Year's Eve countdown begins, the crowd falls silent. When the clock strikes midnight, custom dictates that every Brazilian woman greet three men before she greets another woman. The same holds true for the men— they must greet three women before they acknowledge another man. This custom is meant to ensure that the person will be lucky in love.

Afterward, everyone welcomes the new year with loud shouts of laughter and joy. People throw themselves into each other's arms, hugging and kissing and wishing each other *Feliz Ano Novo,* which is Portuguese for "Happy New Year." Spectacular fireworks displays can be seen—and heard—outside. Church bells ring in the new year, and shrill blasts from car horns and sirens add to the joyful din. From every direction, Roman candles shoot high into the sky, firecrackers bang, and brilliant flares light up the night. The singing and dancing go on until the wee hours of the dawn—and not till then does anyone even consider going home. After all, it is the Réveillon, and nobody loves a party more than the Brazilians.

For many, the Réveillon is actually the start of Carnival— Brazil's most spectacular festival. Carnival is famous worldwide for its elaborate parades, costume balls, and frenzied, nonstop festivities. Although this grand celebration does not officially start until four days before Lent, many Brazilians get in the Carnival spirit early and celebrate New Year's Eve with the same joyous abandon.

This is especially true at many of Rio de Janeiro's big nightclubs and hotels. Jazz and popular music are played in the early evening, but after the stroke of midnight, the Carnival music begins.

From then till dawn, the people dance to the rhythmic beat of the *samba* and the *lambada*. The samba is the national music of Brazil, while the lambada is a newer rhythm, but both are very popular throughout the country.

On New Year's Eve, however, the vast majority of Brazilians forego these elaborate affairs and opt for something more informal. Many people simply get together at a friend's house for an intimate, private party. They generally dress casually—blue jeans and T-shirts for the men, and often for the women as well. It is very hot in Brazil at this time of year, and loose, lightweight clothing is preferred.

These impromptu parties, which start around 8 or 9 o'clock in the evening, are no less festive than the grandest celebrations in the best Brazilian hotels and nightclubs. Brazilians are masters at creating their own entertainment.

Whenever more than three or four people get together in Brazil, there is always someone who can play a musical instrument, someone who can sing,

Formal New Year's Eve balls in Rio de Janeiro evoke the spirit of the Carnival festivities soon to follow.

and someone who can dance. The festivities start when one person strums a guitar or bursts into song.

Others join in with musical instruments made with whatever is on hand. For example, beans are shaken in a glass jar or an aluminum can, and forks will be tapped against glasses or plates. Even matchboxes can be shaken to add a rhythmic rattle. Many everyday household items are

Spectacular fireworks illuminate the crescent-shaped beaches of Rio de Janeiro.

thus transformed into percussion instruments by the innovative Brazilians. Also, in any gathering, there is always someone who had the foresight to bring along an acoustic guitar, or *violão*. And another partygoer is sure to arrive with a *pandeiro*, or tambourine. This is all Brazilians need to get the music, and the party, started, and everyone joins in the singing. Shyness is the one thing that is frowned upon, and no one is allowed to sit on the sidelines.

Usually the infectious music of the samba proves irresistible, and everyone is soon singing and dancing. There is plenty of wine and champagne to accompany the music. As midnight draws near, the party may move to the beach. A fire is built on the sand, blankets are spread out, and snacks are served. Then champagne is poured, and everyone waits for the fireworks to start. This is a simple yet beautiful way to celebrate the Réveillon—under the stars at the ocean's edge. While only those living along the coast can spend New Year's Eve on the beach, Brazilians everywhere enjoy fireworks displays in local parks or fields.

But nowhere in Brazil are the outdoor celebrations more flamboyant, rambunctious, and just plain awe-inspiring than on Copacabana Beach in Rio de

Brazilian men and women participate in a Candomblé ceremony on New Year's Eve on Copacabana Beach.

Janeiro. To fully grasp the splendor of these festivities, it helps to know something about the area.

Rio de Janeiro enjoys one of the most spectacular geographical settings in the world. The city lies on beautiful Guanabara Bay and is rimmed by sandy beaches and a sparkling blue lagoon. Forested mountains rise to the north and west. Rio de Janeiro has more than 50 miles (80 kilometers) of beaches, including the world-famous Copacabana and Ipanema, names synonymous with sun and surf. And, dominating the landscape, the famous cone-shaped Sugar Loaf Mountain rises from a peninsula in the bay. Then there's the city of Rio itself, ener-

getic, thriving, and devoted to pleasure.

Amid all this natural and artificial beauty, the people of Rio hold one of the nation's largest and most distinctly Brazilian celebrations—the Festival of Iemanjá. This festival is an African spiritualist ceremony that honors Iemanjá, the goddess or queen of the sea.

In Brazil today, African spiritualism is a major religion, and African spiritualist beliefs are intermixed to a large degree with those of the Roman Catholic faith. Followers of these mystical, colorful faiths hold elaborate rituals in which the spirits of the dead are said to communicate with the living through a

A group of followers of Umbanda carry offerings for Iemanjá to the sea.

medium, or living person. Spiritualism was originally brought to Brazil by African slaves hundreds of years ago.

African spiritualism in Brazil today includes several different sects. *Candomblé,* reputed to be the "pure" African religion, is found mainly in Bahia, a state in northeastern Brazil often considered the "soul" of Brazil. *Umbanda,* a sect that blends African beliefs and Roman Catholicism, is found mainly in the south and central regions of the country.

Many people who view themselves as Catholics participate in Umbanda or Candomblé rituals. A well-known joke about religion in Brazil says: "In Brazil, 80 per cent of the people are Catholic—and the remaining 90 per cent are Umbandists." This reflects the degree to which

African spiritualist beliefs, once forbidden by Europeans, have gained acceptance in Brazil.

The Festival of Iemanjá may be called an Umbanda ritual, since it combines African and Catholic beliefs. Over the centuries, belief in the goddess Iemanjá has become intertwined with devotion to the Virgin Mary. In pictures and statues, Iemanjá is often depicted much like Christ's mother, dressed in a white gown with a blue robe draped over her head. On New Year's Eve, a colorful celebration is held in Iemanjá's honor. Early in the morning on December 31, hundreds of thousands of her followers gather along the shore at Copacabana Beach. Many people who do not subscribe to the African religions nevertheless turn out for this unusual and incredibly beautiful celebration that lasts till dawn the next day.

For believers, it is a time to give thanks to Iemanjá for all the blessings of the past year and to ask for her good will during the upcoming twelve months. As many as 200,000 celebrants may flock to Copacabana Beach carrying candles and flowers. Almost everyone is dressed in white—the color of prosperity, peace, and good luck. Many of the women wear billowing white skirts adorned with ruffles and lace and wrap white turbans around their heads. Others wear simpler white robes. Flowers may be worn as necklaces or used to adorn the hair. Sometimes the person actually performing the ritual to Iemanjá is dressed in blue.

Worshipers of the goddess Iemanjá place lighted candles in the sand on the beach in São Paulo.

As night falls, thousands of white candles are placed in the sand, turning the famous crescent-shaped bay of Copacabana Beach into a shimmering carpet of light. Drums begin to roll. Believers dance, sing, and convulse when, according to myth, Iemanjá enters their bodies and possesses them.

Everybody, believers and nonbelievers alike, pays tribute to Iemanjá by bringing her gifts. Iemanjá is a vain creature who likes to receive jewelry, mirrors, flowers, and money. Often, Brazilians put their gifts in little wooden boats—some painted white and up to two or three feet (60 to 90 centimeters) long—and then cast them out to sea. According to legend, if your gift floats out to sea, Iemanjá finds it acceptable and you will have a good year. If your gift washes ashore, however, it is not a good sign, and the following year will not be a happy one. Usually the waves wash all the gifts out to sea, and Brazilians go home happy and relaxed, confident that the new year will be a good one.

Of course, to gain Iemanjá's favor, it is necessary to give her generous gifts—a stingy offering simply will not do. So, more often than not, the little boats are laden with fine combs, brushes, bracelets, earrings, and perfume—gifts that a proud, beautiful woman would like to receive. Iemanjá is also given expensive wines, as well as bouquets of white roses, lilies, and other flowers. Sometimes boats are weighed down with bananas, grapes, pineapples, watermelon, and other tropical fruits intended to please the fickle Iemanjá.

At the stroke of midnight, when Iemanjá receives her gifts, thousands of people run into the ocean carrying their presents. Some simply toss their gifts into the foamy waters, while others cast them forth in the wooden boats. Then, with great joy and exuberance, the people run into the water, clothes and all, allowing the waves to splash them seven times. According to tradition, you can ask Iemanjá for a favor or make a wish each time a wave hits you. To some this may seem to be sheer superstition, but to others it is lots of fun and just might bring good luck and prosperity in the coming year.

Some Brazilians say that if you do not believe in Candomblé or Umbanda before you go to the festival of Iemanjá, you will believe in them afterward. It's hard to resist the raw energy and universal joy of this event.

As if all this were not enough, the night sky, usually

peaceful, suddenly roars from its slumber with the sounds and lights of a hundred fireworks. To everyone's delight, the big hotels along Copacabana Beach compete with one another to see who can put on the most impressive display. The end result is at least half an hour of bursting, brilliant fireworks.

In recent years, Rio's Festival of Iemanjá has been imitated by other coastal cities interested in attracting more tourist business. However, none of the others can match the glorious spectacle at Copacabana Beach. Every year, people come from every part of Brazil and from all over the world to witness this event.

No matter where the Festival of Iemanjá is held, the dancing and music continue long into the night. Some of the celebrants do not leave the beaches till early dawn. When they do go home, exhausted, they may sleep well into the next day.

On New Year's Eve in Brazil, another popular event, known as the *Corrida de São Silvestre* (Saint Sylvester's Race), takes place. The race, held in downtown São Paulo, is an international marathon that attracts thousands of runners every year. No special qualifications are required to enter. Every man, woman, and youth age 16 and up is welcome, and the handicapped can also participate.

The streets of São Paulo overflow with scores of runners competing in the Corrida de São Silvestre.

The Corrida de São Silvestre, first held in 1924, became an international race in 1945. The marathon, which starts and ends on Avenida Paulista, São Paulo's main avenue, is a circular race (a race in which the runners start and end at the same point). The participants run slightly more than 8 miles (13,500 meters), almost twice as far as the original length of the race.

Thousands gather eagerly to take part in the event or cheer on the runners. Participants may have prepared for weeks or even months—rising in the early dawn and running 1 mile (1.6 kilometers) a day to get in shape for the marathon. Many have used every spare moment to jog, exercise, and work out so that they will have the stamina to go the entire distance. Still others are professional runners who have traveled far to compete in this event. Then there are those who decide to run at the last minute and, unless they are in very good physical condition, will find it difficult to keep up with the pros and seasoned runners.

Friends and relatives also turn out in droves to watch their runners and cheer them on. Avenida Paulista is awash in a sea of people at this time, and streets along the race's route are blocked off to accommodate the runners and crowds.

The runners—highly visible in bright-colored shorts, tank tops, and professional running shoes—stretch, jump, jog in place, and do last-minute warm-up exercises before the race officially begins. The energy level is high as starting time draws near.

Finally, the signal is given and the runners are off with a joyful roar. Like horses penned up too long, they bolt from the starting point, breaking through the fragile ribbon. Soon they are all sprinting at a steady pace, while the crowd, caught up in the excitement, shouts encouragement. Great athletes from all over the world can be seen jogging next to normally sedentary businesspeople.

When the race is over, the winners receive prizes. Awards are given to the first man and the first woman who finish the race, and to the runners-up.

Although this marathon still draws tremendous crowds, the race has undergone a change in recent years that has proved unpopular with many Brazilians. Since its inception, Saint Sylvester's race had always started exactly at the stroke of midnight on New Year's Eve. Recently, however, the starting time was changed, and now the marathon is held in the afternoon.

Runners and residents of São Paulo have criticized the change. Runners preferred to race in the cooler early morning hours, rather than in the heat of the afternoon sun. And many bystanders enjoyed the

This costumed partygoer, festively dressed for New Year's, brings to mind the participants of Carnival.

combined festivities of Saint Sylvester's Race and New Year's Eve.

Over the years, however, Saint Sylvester's Race has become a popular televised event, with millions of viewers watching it at home. It was thought that more viewers would be able to see the race if it was run in the afternoon, and indeed, this has proved to be the case.

Whether or not Saint Sylvester's Race will ever move back to its traditional time slot remains to be seen, but for now, the Corrida de São Silvestre is held in the afternoon. Of course, the new scheduling al-lows people to enjoy the race in the afternoon and take part in night-time festivities too.

There is much to do on New Year's Eve in Brazil—many parties to attend and activities to enjoy. No one gets much sleep on New Year's Eve. And why should they? It is the Réveillon, and the very word *réveillon* means "to awaken the new year." If the new year was ever asleep, it is surely awake now—after Brazilians have finished celebrating it as only Brazilians could.

Chapter 5

End-of-the-Year Celebrations

What do Brazilians do after all the excitement of Christmas and New Year's Eve is over? Do they relax and unwind? Well—yes, but not for long. In this South American country, the celebrations continue for up to a week after Christmas and New Year's Eve have come and gone.

On New Year's Day, for example, a boat parade honors *Nossa Senhora dos Navegantes* (Our Lady of Sailors). Then there is the *Folia de Reis* (Festival of Kings), a month-long religious festival celebrated in rural areas of central Brazil. There is also the *Congada,* an end-of-the-year festival held in many Brazilian cities. Then there are the *pastoris,* theater productions of the Nativity scene that are descendants of old Portuguese traditions. And finally there is the *Bumba-meu-Boi,* a play based on a folk tale about a slain ox.

While most of these affairs are local celebrations that reflect the customs of the people living in a particular region, the boat procession in honor of Our Lady of Sailors is celebrated in many areas of Brazil. Held on New Year's Day, this gala fête marks the time when seafarers everywhere pay tribute to Nossa Senhora dos Navegantes, who watches over them. This Roman Catholic ceremony is widely attended in Brazil, not only for its religious significance, but also for its entertainment value. It is a

A statue of Nossa Senhora dos Navegantes is carried through the streets of Juàzeiro do Norte, in the state of Ceara.

In the city of Porto Alegre, crowds of onlookers gather to witness the procession of boats honoring Our Lady of Sailors.

flamboyant, lively affair that attracts viewers of all ages.

On New Year's Day, hundreds of boats of every size and shape appear on the nation's rivers and coastal waters. Nearly every kind of boat is represented—from simple schooners and fireboats to luxury yachts, from sailboats to motorboats and speedboats. And every one is dressed for the occasion—festooned with flowers, bright with banners and Brazilian flags, and often adorned with colored lights. Brazilians crowd the shoreline by the thousands, all eager to get the best view. They spread out their blankets, break open the cold drinks, and enjoy the parade. The weather is usu-

ally ideal for this occasion—bright, hot, and sunny—and children especially enjoy this colorful water parade. It is a magnificent sight, with one beautifully decorated boat after another floating leisurely by. It is not unusual for 100 boats or more to take part in this procession. In no order whatsoever—the humble schooner next to the elegant yacht—they sail proudly by. Each boat manuevers at will, finding its own place with no thought of an orderly line-up. For several hours they sail side-by-side, each one offering up thanks to Nossa Senhora dos Navegantes for protecting it at sea during the year.

To ask for her blessing and protection during the upcoming year as well, a Catholic ceremony is held at the end of the parade. The boat processions end near a church, preferably one called Nossa Senhora dos Navegantes. A street procession begins where the boat parade left off. Several Brazilians carry a statue of Nossa Senhora dos Navegantes to the church on a platform, accompanied by a cheering and joyful crowd. Many people sing songs and hymns in honor of this very special day for those who sail the sea.

As the street procession makes its way toward the church, the statue is carried up to the altar with great ceremony. The statue of Our Lady of Sailors is blessed, and a special Catholic ritual is performed in her honor. Onlookers crowd the church to witness the blessing of Nossa Senhora dos Navegantes. After the ceremony, some people may linger, singing and dancing in the streets, while others go back to their boats and sail home—content in the knowledge that it will be another safe year at sea, now that they are once again under the protection of Our Lady of Sailors.

The feast of Our Lady of Sailors has always been an important celebration in Brazil, for several reasons. First, Brazil was originally discovered by Portuguese seafarers, and second, most Brazilians still live along the coast, so boating and sailing are a big part of their lives. It is only natural, then, that they would seek the protection of Our Lady of Sailors against the sometimes treacherous Atlantic Ocean and the mighty Amazon River.

In the rural areas of central Brazil at this time of year, people celebrate a quite different tradition. Known as the *Folia de Reis* (the Festival of Kings), it is both an end-of-the-year celebration and a tribute to *os Tres Reis Magos* (the Three Wise Men). In addition, the Folia de Reis is a time when each village or town pays homage to its patron saint. In Brazil, nearly every city and village has elected a particular saint to watch over their city, and custom dictates that homage be paid to that saint at this time.

The Folia de Reis festival officially starts on December 24th and ends on January 6th, Three Kings' Day. In some areas, however, the singing and dancing may begin as early as December 20th and last until January 20th, St. Sebastian's Day.

During the month-long festival, religious groups known as Reisados parade through the streets, playing musical instruments and singing songs. These religious groups are made up of local celebrants, and it often seems as though every man, woman, and child in the village has joined in the revelry. The Reisados put on a show that rivals some of the best theatrical presentations in Brazil. Wearing bright costumes and masks of almost every variety and color, they strut, jump, and leap into the air as they parade down the street. The masks—sometimes scary, sometimes animallike—are almost always innovative creations of the revelers themselves. Some are elaborate creations featuring feathers and face-paint, while others are simple masks made of paper or plastic that can be easily taken off. Even the children wear masks or have their faces made up to disguise their true identities. And some revelers wear elaborate cone-shaped hats and other colorful attire.

Still other Reisados go a step further and dress up as clowns. The clowns interact with the bystanders, playfully entertaining them, and sometimes teasing the crowd into joining the parade, or coaxing people to sing and dance with them.

The Reisados use a wide variety of musical instruments during the Folia de Reis. Many people play a *pandeiro* (tambourine), *zabumba* (big, round drum), or *tamborim* (a very small drum played with a long stick). Others may squeeze a lively sound from a *sanfona,* a small accordion. In addition, there are always men and boys who add the sweet music of a Brazilian violin, known as a *rabeca,* to the street parade. Everyone plays with great exuberance and often with great skill. The Brazilians are a very musical people, and no one would think of standing on the sidelines when they could join in the festivities and start dancing and singing themselves.

During every Folia de Reis procession, no matter how small, there is always an *estandarte,* or saint's flag. Sometimes several estandartes are carried aloft in one procession. Usually it is a great honor to carry the estandarte, and every village has its own unique saint's flag.

The Reisados gradually make their way through the village, stopping at every house to ask for donations to prepare for the *Santos Reis* (the Saints' Kings' Party) on January 6th. The Reisados are given food and drink at each house they visit. Sometimes these masked revelers travel on horseback through the countryside to reach their next destination. Other times they go on foot.

At the first house they visit when they arrive at a village, they are served food that is the specialty of that region or town. Typical Brazilian favorites may also be served, such as *feijoada* and *churrasco.* Feijoada, the national dish of Brazil, was originally created by Brazilian slaves. Black beans are the basis of this dish, and dried beef, bacon, salted pork, ox tongue, and pig's ears may be added. The mixture is spiced with garlic, bay leaves, and onions, and is often accompanied by white rice, farofa, kale, and oranges.

Churrasco too is a very popular Brazilian dish. It consists of a variety of barbecued meats.

Afterward, there is more singing and dancing. Often the songs are about the birth of Christ. In spite of all the merrymaking and theatrical overtones, the primarily religious nature of this festival is apparent. Whenever the Folia de Reis takes place on Christmas Eve, the Reisados take part in a procession with four distinctly religious parts.

The first of these is the tradition of attending midnight Mass on Christmas Eve. At exactly midnight, the Reisados offer up

Reisados, some in costume and others playing musical instruments, wind through the streets in a colorful procession.

a song in front of the altar or the Nativity scene. As they approach the altar, the Reisados make the sign of the cross and kneel down in reverence. They then sing a Christmas hymn, and afterward, as they are leaving the church, they join in a farewell chant. Their contribution adds considerable charm to the Missa do Galo and is enjoyed by all.

The second part of this ritual procession is called The Chant of the Door. The revelers go from house to house during Christmas night to awaken and greet the people. According to tradition, the head of the household is the only one who may open the door to the Reisados, and he may do this only after they have finished their first song or chant. There are two exceptions to these rules, however. If it is raining, or if the door is already open, the Reisados need not wait for a formal invitation—they can just walk right in! They usually enter a house singing and dancing, to the delight of the entire family. They are expected and welcome guests, and an abundance of food and drink has already been laid out for them. The Reisados, who have worked up quite an appetite after all that singing and

Participants of a Congada celebration, wearing hats with long, colorful streamers, sing and dance as they parade through the city streets.

dancing, eat heartily from the feast set before them. Sometimes they even receive small gifts for their efforts.

The next part of this procession is known as The Chant of Saluting the Stable. The Reisados go to the village stable, or presépio, where they kneel down and pay their respects to the baby Jesus. Then everyone joins in a short chant. After the religious traditions have been observed, everyone breaks into a sort of tap dance known as the *Lundu*—the fourth and last part of the procession, and one that is obviously enjoyed by all. The Lundu is a happy dance, perhaps the most free-spirited and energetic part of the Christmas Eve procession. The Folia de Reis may attract anywhere from a dozen people to more than a thousand, depending on the size of the village or town.

Another festive celebration similar to the Folia de Reis is the *Congada*. Like the Folia de Reis, the Congada is a religious festival that commemorates the end of the year. However, it differs from the Folia de Reis in that the Congada is celebrated primarily in the cities rather than the rural areas. The Congada is also an occasion when a city's patron saint is honored, and it is every bit as flamboyant, lively, and free-spirited as the Folia de Reis. The celebrations include a street procession made up of musicians, singers, and dancers. Many of the same musical instruments are used, and many of the same songs are sung. Also like the Folia de Reis, crowds of people participate in the Congada. Men and women may wear straw hats with multicolored streamers so thick and long that they cover the wearer almost from head to toe. Many people play a musical instrument as they make their way through the city.

Like rural people at the Folia de Reis, urban dwellers carry the estandarte or saint's flag of the city's patron saint, and anywhere from one to a dozen estandartes are carried in the procession. City people enjoy their Congada every bit as much as rural folks enjoy their Folia de Reis, and thousands of people turn out for the celebration. Hundreds more actually participate, including many children. This combination end-of-the-year and patron saint's celebration is especially enjoyable for young children—a time to wear colorful hats, dress up, and participate in a musical parade. Even those who don't actively join in the Congada enjoy watching it from the sidelines. There is also a delightful variety of food

A young boy wears the costume of the bull, the star in the Bumba-meu-Boi celebrations of Brazil's Northeast.

and drink available at the Congada. At the end of the festivities, a huge dinner is prepared and served for all the musicians and other participants. Again, the dishes offered include the specialties of the city or region, as well as other popular Brazilian dishes. The Congada, like the Folia de Reis, is an exotic and playful affair—the kind of religious festival that could only be found in Brazil.

Another event unique to Brazilian culture is a sort of folklore theater known as the *pastoril.* Derived from old Portuguese traditions that celebrated the Nativity, the pastorils today are theatrical presentations that revolve around the *pastoras,* or shepherdesses, who have the lead roles. The pastoras sing songs and perform dances that may be either religious or secular in nature. For instance, a dance called "The Seduction" portrays the devil trying to influence a little shepherdess toward evil. Then there are three free-spirited dances known as the "Butterfly Dance," the "Gypsy Woman Dance," and the "Ribbons Dance." The pastoras may also sing a series of songs known as the *Chulas.* Like everything else in Brazil, these folklore productions are colorful, spontaneous, and uninhibited. They are performed throughout the Christmas season in

many regions of Brazil, and are much enjoyed by the Brazilian people.

Perhaps the most significant festivity of the season is the *Bumba-meu-Boi,* or Beating of the Bull. This theatrical event takes place throughout Brazil, and is especially elaborate in the Northeast. Of all the events of the holiday season, the Bumba-meu-Boi is the one that most clearly shows the blending of the African, Indian, and Portuguese influences on the Brazilian culture.

The Bumba-meu-Boi is a story about a bull. There are many variations of the story, depending on the region in which it is performed. In one version, the bull, who dances and leaps among the audience, is killed by a cowboy to prepare a meal for his lover. When the cattle owner discovers that his bull is missing, he demands that the cowboy produce it, threatening to kill the cowboy if the ox is not returned. A folk doctor, called a *curador,* revives the bull and saves the cowboy's life.

The bull costume is a structure made of wood, wire, and cloth. Velvet or flowery cotton covers a mesh foundation. The bull's head is usually made of painted papier-mâché, and flowers or ribbons often adorn the horns. The play lasts for several hours. Costumes may be extremely elaborate, and music, rhyme, and dance are often incorporated. In some regions, the play is known by another name, such as *Boi-de-Máscaras, Boi-de-Orquestra,* or *Folguendo do Boi.*

With the arrival of Three Kings' Day on January 6th, the Christmas season in Brazil is officially over. Schools and businesses are closed in observance of this holy day, sometimes called *Epiphany,* which commemorates the visit of the Magi to the holy infant Jesus. In some parts of Brazil, an old Portuguese custom is still practiced on the eve of Epiphany. On this night, children put their shoes beside the window or outside the door, hoping to find them filled with treats in the morning. Usually they are not disappointed. According to myth, it is the Three Wise Men who fill the shoes with goodies, though cold logic might suggest that this task falls to the parents. Regardless, on January 6th, children find their shoes filled with chocolates and other goodies—a fitting end to the Christmas season.

Three Kings' Day is also the time when many Brazilians take down their Christmas trees and presépios. Street decorations and Christmas lights are dismantled, and shopping malls and boutiques replace their Christmas displays with something new. The Christmas season is over. There are no more end-of-the-year celebrations, no more special Christmas observances to keep, and no more rowdy pastoris.

This does not mean, however, that the festivities in Brazil are over. On the contrary, now that the Christmas season is over, there is only one thing for Brazilians to do: start preparing for the next big celebration—Carnival.

Carnival is the culmination of all the summer festivities—including Christmas, New Year's Eve, and the various end-of-the-year celebrations. This four-day extravaganza is famous the world over for the sheer size and extravagance of its street parades, costumes, and balls—to say nothing of the nonstop singing and dancing. Although it won't take place until late February, Carnival is a perfect way to end the summer season, and it gives everyone something to look forward to now that Christmas is over. And in Brazil, everyone needs at least one more festival to look forward to. After all, what is life without a celebration?

Crafts

Just as Brazilian Christmas traditions have been influenced by those in the United States and Europe, Brazilian Christmas crafts share many similarities with those found in America and in countries throughout Europe.

Decorative Reindeer

This reindeer can be used as a standing table decoration or as a hanging ornament for your Christmas tree or window. You might also use one or more reindeer to decorate a Christmas wreath.

To make a standing reindeer:

1. Using tracing paper, trace the pattern on the following page. Cut out the pattern from the tracing paper, and lay it down on construction paper. Trace around the edges of the pattern with a pencil. Repeat the process so that you have two bodies and two antlers. (For variety, you may want to use different colors of construction paper for the antlers and the bodies.)

2. Cut out the patterns on the construction paper.

3. Place glue on one of the body shapes where shown on the pattern. Note that you will be placing glue only on the top part of the body. Join the two reindeer bodies together so that they match up.

4. Glue the antlers to the top of the reindeer's head. You should place one antler on each side of the head, with one of the antlers slightly to the right of the other.

Materials
- tracing paper
- pencil
- heavy, colorful construction paper
- crayons or markers
- scissors
- glue
- narrow ribbon
- glitter
- cotton (optional)
- sequins (optional)
- hole punch
- 3" x 5" index card or construction paper cut into a 3" x 5" rectangle

5. When the glue is dry, you can decorate the reindeer, one side at a time. For example, you might want to outline the antlers with glue and spread glitter over them, or you could use crayons or markers to color in some details, such as the reindeer's eyes and nose. You could also glue a small piece of white cotton to the tail, or glue a red sequin to the nose.

6. If you would like to personalize the reindeer, you can use glue to write your name or a friend's name on the body, then sprinkle glitter over the glue.

7. When both sides of the reindeer have been decorated, tie a narrow ribbon around the reindeer's neck.

glue

8. To attach the reindeer to the base, fold its feet at the fold line shown on the pattern. The construction paper should fold outward. Place a dab of glue at the bottom surface of each foot, and attach the feet to a 3" x 5" index card or the precut construction paper rectangle. Your reindeer is now ready to take its place on any table.

1/4"

fold

fold

To make a hanging reindeer:
1. Follow steps 1 and 2 listed under the heading "To make a standing reindeer," but cut two antlers and only one body.

2. Assemble and decorate the reindeer as described in steps 3 through 7.

3. Punch a hole in the reindeer's body, and tie a narrow ribbon through the hole to make a hanger.

Gourd Noisemaker*

Materials
- small dried gourd, 2" to 3" in diameter
- wooden dowel, 3/8" in diameter
- small pebbles or pieces of gravel
- wood glue
- enamel paint and small brushes, sequins, or construction paper to decorate gourd
- ruler
- hand drill and 1/4" bit
- craft knife
- craft saw
- 2 cans or jars

1. Using the hand drill, drill a 1/4" hole in the bottom of the gourd, making sure not to lose any of the seeds inside the gourd. If there are not enough seeds inside the gourd to make a good rattling sound, add a few small pebbles or pieces of gravel.

*This craft should be made with the supervision and help of an adult.

Tinsel-Tailed Tropical Birds

Materials
- tracing paper
- construction paper
- scissors
- pencil
- hole punch
- crayons or markers
- glitter
- sequins
- glue
- tinsel
- narrow ribbon

1. Using tracing paper, trace one of the patterns. Cut out the pattern from the tracing paper, and lay it down on a sheet of construction paper. Trace around the edges of the pattern with a pencil.

2. Cut out the pattern from the construction paper. Punch out the holes shown on the pattern.

3. Decorate the bird with crayons or markers, glitter, sequins, or layers of construction paper shaped like feathers. You can decorate both sides of the bird the same or different. When done, cut out the bird.

4. Apply glue to the insides of the front and back of the bird. Fold the bird in half along the dotted line, pressing the halves together. Allow to dry.

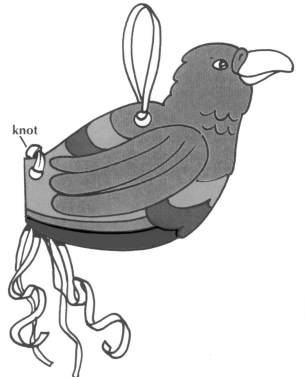

knot

5. Pull several strands of tinsel halfway through the tail hole and knot at top.

6. Thread a piece of narrow ribbon through the top hole on the bird and knot, making a loop by which you can hang the bird.

7. Repeat steps 1 through 6 using the other pattern, or create patterns of your own to make a whole flock of tropical birds!

70

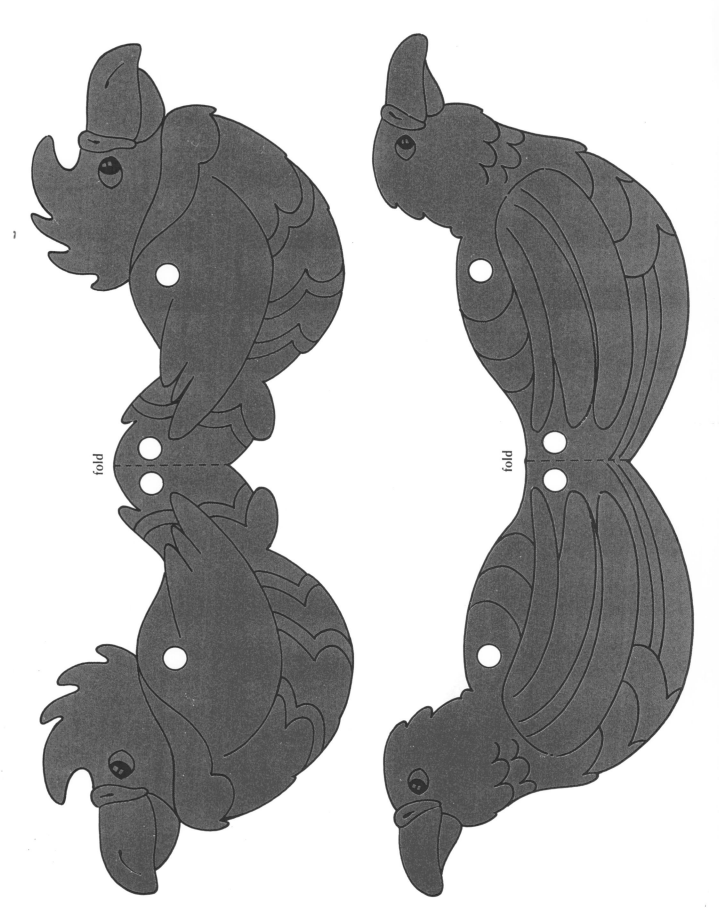

fold

fold

Recipes

Smoked and Fresh Meat with Accompaniments (Feijoada Completa)

A 3-lb. smoked beef tongue
1 lb. corned spareribs, if available
1/2 lb. jerked or dried beef, in 1 piece
1/2 lb. *chorizo* or other smoked spiced pork sausage
1/2 lb. fresh breakfast-type pork sausage
1 fresh pig's foot, if available
3-1/2 quarts water
4 cups dried black beans
1/4 lb. lean bacon, in 1 piece with the rind removed
1 lb. lean beef chuck, in 1 piece
1/2 lb. Canadian-style bacon, in 1 piece
2 tbsp. lard
1-1/2 cups coarsely chopped onions
1 tbsp. finely chopped garlic

3 medium tomatoes, peeled, seeded, and coarsely chopped, or substitute 1 cup chopped, drained, canned Italian plum tomatoes
2 bottled Tabasco™ peppers, drained, seeded, and finely chopped
1 tsp. salt
1/2 tsp. freshly ground black pepper
Farofa de Manteiga (see recipe, page 74)
Arroz Brasileiro (see recipe, page 74)
Couve à Mineira (see recipe, page 75)
Môlho de Pimenta e Limão (see recipe, page 75)
5 large oranges, peeled and thinly sliced or cut into chunks

The Meats:

Place the tongue, spareribs, and jerked beef in separate pots, and cover the meats with cold water. Soak them overnight.

Precook the meats in the following fashion: Drain the tongue, cover it with fresh water, and bring to a boil over high heat. Partially cover the pan, reduce the heat, and simmer for 2-1/2 hours. The tongue should be kept covered with water; if it boils away, add more boiling water. Remove the tongue from the water and let it cool slightly.

Then skin it with a sharp knife, cutting away the fat, bones, and gristle at its base.

Drain the jerked beef, cover it with fresh water, and bring to a boil. Reduce the heat and simmer uncovered for 30 minutes; drain and set aside.

Drain the spareribs, add the smoked sausage, fresh sausage, and pig's foot, and cover with fresh water. Bring to a boil, reduce the heat to low, and simmer uncovered for 15 minutes. Drain and set the meats aside.

The Beans:

In a heavy 12-quart casserole or a large soup pot, bring 3 quarts of water to a boil over high heat. Drop in the beans and boil them briskly for 2 minutes. Turn off the heat and let the beans soak for 1 hour. Then add the peeled tongue, jerked beef, spareribs, pig's foot, and lean bacon. Bring to a boil, reduce the heat to low, cover and simmer for 1 hour. Check the water in the pot occasionally. It should cook away somewhat, leaving the beans moist and slightly soupy; but if the beans get too dry, add some boiling water. Preheat the oven to 250°. Transfer the tongue to a large heatproof platter, cover it with foil, and place it in the oven to keep warm. Add the chuck to the pot, and continue cooking the beans and meat for 1 hour. Finally, add the smoked and fresh sausage and Canadian bacon, and cook for 30 minutes. When the meats are tender, remove them from the pot and place them in the oven on the platter with the tongue. Skim the fat from the surface of the beans and remove the pot from the heat.

The Sauce:

In a heavy 8- to 10-inch skillet, melt the lard over moderate heat. Add the onions and garlic, and cook, stirring frequently, for 5 minutes, or until the onions are soft and transparent but not brown. Stir in the tomatoes, Tabasco peppers, salt, and black pepper, and simmer for 5 minutes. With a slotted spoon, remove 2 cups of beans from the casserole and add them to the skillet. Mash them thoroughly into the onion mixture, moistening them with 2 cups of the bean liquid as you mash. Stirring occasionally, simmer the sauce over low heat for 15 minutes, or until it becomes thick. With a rubber spatula, scrape the sauce into the pot and cook over low heat, stirring occasionally, for 20 minutes.

To Assemble:

With a large, sharp knife, slice the beef tongue, jerked beef, lean bacon, chuck, Canadian bacon, spareribs, and pig's foot into serving pieces, and separate the smoked and fresh sausages. Transfer the beans to a serving bowl. Traditionally, all the meats are presented on one large, heated platter with the sliced tongue in the center, the fresh meat on one side, the smoked meats on the other. Present the beans, *farofa, couve, môlho, arroz,* and orange slices in separate bowls or platters. Serves 8 to 10.

From FOODS OF THE WORLD
Recipes: Latin American Cooking
© 1968 Time-Life Books Inc.

Toasted Manioc Meal (*Farofa de Manteiga*)

2 tbsp. butter
1/2 large peeled onion, thinly sliced
1 egg, lightly beaten
1-1/3 cups manioc meal
1 tsp. salt
1 tbsp. finely chopped parsley
4 pimento-stuffed olives, cut crosswise into 1/4-inch slices (optional)
2 to 4 hard-cooked eggs, cut in half lengthwise

In a heavy 8- to 10-inch skillet, heat the butter over moderate heat, tipping the pan to coat the bottom evenly. Drop in the onion slices and cook them, stirring constantly, for 5 minutes, or until they are soft and transparent but not brown. Reduce the heat to low and—still stirring constantly—pour in the egg. The egg will coagulate in seconds. Slowly stir in the manioc meal and cook, stirring frequently, for 8 minutes, or until the meal becomes golden. Watch carefully for any sign of burning. Stir in the salt and parsley. Serve hot or cooled to room temperature. The *farofa* may be garnished in either case with olives and hard-cooked eggs. Serves 8 to 10.

From FOODS OF THE WORLD
Recipes: Latin American Cooking
© 1968 Time-Life Books Inc.

Rice with Tomatoes and Onions (*Arroz Brasileiro*)

1/4 cup olive oil
1 large onion, thinly sliced
3 cups raw long-grain rice
3 cups boiling chicken stock, fresh or canned
3 cups boiling water
2 medium tomatoes, peeled, seeded, and coarsely chopped,
    or substitute 2/3 cup chopped, drained, canned Italian plum tomatoes
1 tsp. salt

In a heavy 3- to 4-quart saucepan, heat the oil over moderate heat for 30 seconds, tipping the pan to coat the bottom evenly. Add the onion and cook, stirring constantly, for 5 minutes, or until it is soft and transparent but not brown. Pour in the rice and stir for 2 to 3 minutes, until all the grains are coated with oil. Do not let the rice brown. Add the stock, water, tomatoes, and salt, and return to a boil, still stirring. Cover the pan and reduce the heat to its lowest point. Simmer for 20 minutes, or until the rice has absorbed all the liquid. If the rice must wait, drape the pan loosely with a towel and keep it warm in a preheated 250° oven. Serves 8 to 10.

From FOODS OF THE WORLD
Recipes: Latin American Cooking
© 1968 Time-Life Books Inc.

Shredded Kale Greens (Couve à Mineira)

5 lbs. kale greens, or substitute
  5 lbs. collard greens
3/4 cup bacon fat
1-1/2 tsp. salt

Wash the kale or collard greens under cold running water. With a sharp knife, trim away any bruised or blemished spots and cut the leaves from their tough stems. Shred the leaves into 1/4-inch strips. In a large pot, bring 4 quarts of water to a boil over high heat. Drop in the greens and cook them uncovered for 3 minutes. Then drain them in a colander, pressing down on the greens with a spoon to extract all their liquid. In a heavy 10- to 12-inch skillet, melt the bacon fat over moderate heat, and, when it is hot, but not smoking, add the greens. Cook, stirring frequently, for 30 minutes, or until the greens are tender, but slightly crisp. Don't let them brown. Stir in the salt and serve at once. If the greens must wait, cover them with foil, and keep them warm in a preheated 250° oven. Serves 8 to 10.

From FOODS OF THE WORLD
Recipes: Latin American Cooking
© 1968 Time-Life Books Inc.

Pepper and Lemon Sauce (Môlho de Pimenta e Limão)

4 bottled Tabasco™ peppers,
  drained and finely chopped
1/2 cup finely chopped onions
1/4 tsp. finely chopped garlic
1/2 cup fresh lemon juice

In a small bowl, combine the peppers, onions, garlic, and lemon juice, and stir until they are well mixed. Marinate, uncovered, at room temperature for an hour before serving, or refrigerate, covered, for as long as 4 hours. Makes about 1 cup.

From FOODS OF THE WORLD
Recipes: Latin American Cooking
© 1968 Time-Life Books Inc.

Neck Stuffing for Roast Turkey, Brazilian Style
(see recipe card)

4 cups manioc meal*
2 tbsp. butter
1 chopped onion
1/2 cup chopped tomatoes
  (optional)
1/4 cup chopped parsley
1 cup giblet broth
1 portion of the reserved giblets
4 or 5 drops Tabasco™ sauce
3 tbsp. butter
1/2 cup stuffed olives
3 chopped hard-boiled eggs

Gently brown manioc meal in the oven. Set aside. Melt butter in a large skillet and sauté onion, tomatoes, and parsley. Add giblets, Tabasco sauce and the other 3 tbsp. of butter. When butter is melted, remove from heat and gradually stir in the browned manioc meal. Add the giblet broth, and mix well until all the meal has been blended, then return to low heat, stirring constantly until mixture is loose. Add olives and chopped eggs, and taste to correct seasoning.

* Manioc meal can be purchased at specialty stores that carry ingredients for cooking Latin American foods. If unavailable, Cream of Wheat™ or Farina™ may be substituted.

**Breast Stuffing for
Roast Turkey,
Brazilian Style**
(see recipe card)

1/4 cup chopped bacon
1/2 cup chopped onion
1/4 cup minced parsley
2 cloves of garlic, minced
1 cup giblet broth
1 portion of the reserved giblets
6 cups of bread cubes soaked in
   3/4 cup of milk
1/2 cup chopped tomatoes

Fry bacon in skillet and re-move the fat. Add onion, garlic, parsley, and tomato. When brown, cover with the broth and bring to a boil. Press through a sieve and add the giblets and bread. Mix well with a fork. Season to taste.

**Pineapple/Lime
Cooler (*Refresco de
Lima e Abacaxi*)**

8 tbsp. freshly squeezed lime
   juice
1-1/2 cups pineapple juice
8 ice cubes
3 cups chilled club soda
2 orange slices

Divide the pineapple juice into equal servings in four tall beverage glasses. Add 2 tbsp.

of lime juice and 2 ice cubes to each glass. Pour equal amounts of club soda in each glass to fill. Cut each orange slice in half, and cut the center of each half-slice partway to the peel. Hang one orange piece on the rim of each glass to garnish. Serves four.

Lullaby for Baby Jesus

Repousa tranquilo O meigo Jesus

Translated from the Portuguese
English version by R.H.

Brazilian
Arranged by R.H.

Tenderly and smoothly

1. Sleep qui-et-ly, my Je-sus, Now close Thy dear eyes. A-
2. The shep-herds leave their flocks and come, They bring Thee their love, While

bove Thee shine God's count-less stars, Like dia-monds in the sky. Be-
an-gels of our Fath'r in heav'n Re-joice in song a-bove. From

side Thy bed, a man-ger crude, Where cat-tle have fed, Thy
far a-way the Wise Men three Their treas-ures do bring. The

Moth-er stands in watch-ful prayer, And strokes Thy bless-ed head.
whole wide world be-fore Thee kneels, My Je-sus, lit-tle King.

Away in a Manger

Na Manjedoura

Letra atribuída a Martinho Lutero, 1535
Mel. atribuída a Martinho Lutero, 1530
Trad. de Adelina Cerqueira Leite, 1947

1. Sem lar e sem berço, dei - ta-do em ca-pim, Os bra - ços mo - ven-do, Je - sus cha - ma as - sim. Es - tre - las a - brin-do as cor - ti - nas dos céus Es - pi - am na gruta o Me - ni - no que é Deus.

2. O gado mugindo, põe-se Êle a
    sorrir,
    A nós prenunciando um alegre
    porvir!
    Eu te amo, Jesus; vem meu sono
    velar
    E fica ao meu lado até o dia
    clarear.

3. Conduz os meus passos na trilha
    do bem
    E teu amor dá-me, eu te peço
    também.
    Vigia as crianças, prepara o seu
    lar
    Nos céus onde irão junto a Ti
    habitar.

From *Cânticos do Natal*, selected and annotated by Henriqueta Rosa Fernandes Braga, ©1954

Silent Night

Noite de paz!

José Mohr, 1818
Adapt. da Comissão do Hinário,* 1945

Francisco Xavier Gruber, 1818

Andante

1. Noi - te de paz! Noi - te de a mor! Tu - do dor-me em der-re-dor.

En-tre os as-tros que es- par-gem a luz, Pro - cla-man-do o Me - ni - no Je-sus,

Bri - lha a es - tre - la da paz! Bri - lha a es - tre - la da paz!

2. Noite de paz! Noite de amor!
   Nas campinas ao pastor,
   Lindos anjos, mandados por Deus,
   Anunciam a nova dos céus —
   Nasce o bom Salvador,
   Nasce o bom Salvador.

3. Noite de paz! Noite de amor!
   Oh! Que belo resplendor
   Ilumina o Menino Jesus!
   No presépio do mundo eis a luz,
   Sol de eterno fulgor!
   Sol de eterno fulgor!

*Por gentileza da Confederação Evangélica do Brasil.
From *Cânticos do Natal*, selected and annotated by Henriqueta Rosa Fernandes Braga, ©1954

Acknowledgements

Cover: © Luiz C. Marigo from Peter Arnold
© NelsonToledo, IKSO-Reflexo

2: © Artur Ikissima, Abril Imagens
6: © Luiz Dantas, Abril Imagens
8: © Oscar Cabral, Abril Imagens
11: © Carlos Namba, Abril Imagens
12: © Ricardo Azoury, IKSO-Reflexo
14: © Ricardo Chaves, Abril Imagens
15: © Jorge Rosenberg, Fotograma
16: © Renato De Souza, Abril Imagens
17: © Nelson Toledo, IKSO-Reflexo
18: © Marcelo Vigneron, IKSO-Reflexo
19: © Rivaldo Gomes, IKSO-Reflexo
21: © Luiz Aureliano, Abril Imagens
22: © Nelson Toledo, IKSO-Reflexo
23: © Nelson Toledo, IKSO-Reflexo
25: © Kim-Ir-Sen, IKSO-Reflexo
27: © Luiz Aureliano, Abril Imagens
28: © Marcelo Vigneron, IKSO-Reflexo
30: © Nelson Toledo, IKSO-Reflexo
31: © José Antonio, Abril Imagens
32: © Marcelo Vigneron, IKSO-Reflexo

33: © Marcelo Vigneron, IKSO-Reflexo
34: © Nelson Toledo, IKSO-Reflexo
35: © Nelson Toledo, IKSO-Reflexo
37: © Marcelo Vigneron, IKSO-Reflexo
38: © Tarcisio Mattos, IKSO-Reflexo
40: © Marcelo Vigneron, IKSO-Reflexo
42: © Irmo Celso, Abril Imagens
45: © Ricardo Chvaicer, Abril Imagens
46: © Oscar Cabral, Abril Imagens
47: © Rogerio Reis, IKSO-Reflexo
48: © Pedro Viegas, IKSO-Reflexo
49: © Irmo Celso, Abril Imagens
51: © Rivaldo Gomes, IKSO-Reflexo
53: © Kim-Ir-Sen, IKSO-Reflexo
54: © Julio Bernardes, IKSO-Reflexo
56: © Carlos Namba, Abril Imagens
58: © Emidio Luisi, IKSO-Reflexo
60: © Rosa Gauditano, IKSO-Reflexo
62: © Kim-Ir-Sen, IKSO-Reflexo

Color illustrations: Lydia Halverson
Crafts illustrations: Rick Incrocci